Backyard Bird Watchers

A Bird Watcher's Guide to
SPARROWS

By
Grace Vail

Gareth Stevens
PUBLISHING

Please visit our website, www.garethstevens.com. For a free color catalog of all our high-quality books, call toll free 1-800-542-2595 or fax 1-877-542-2596.

Library of Congress Cataloging-in-Publication Data

Names: Vail, Grace, author.
Title: A bird watcher's guide to sparrows / Grace Vail.
Description: New York : Gareth Stevens Publishing, [2016] | Series: Backyard bird watchers | Includes bibliographical references and index.
Identifiers: LCCN 2015031493 | ISBN 9781482439113 (pbk.) | ISBN 9781482439120 (6 pack) | ISBN 9781482439137 (library bound)
Subjects: LCSH: Sparrows–Identification–Juvenile literature. | Bird watching–Juvenile literature.
Classification: LCC QL696.P262 V35 2016 | DDC 598.8/83–dc23
LC record available at http://lccn.loc.gov/2015031493

First Edition

Published in 2016 by
Gareth Stevens Publishing
111 East 14th Street, Suite 349
New York, NY 10003

Copyright © 2016 Gareth Stevens Publishing

Designer: Laura Bowen
Editor: Therese Shea

Photo credits: Cover, p. 1 (sparrow) Rob Christiaans/Shutterstock.com; cover, pp. 1–32 (paper texture) javarman/Shutterstock.com; cover, pp. 1–32 (footprints) pio3/Shutterstock.com; pp. 4–29 (note paper) totallyPic.com/Shutterstock.com; pp. 4–29 (photo frame, tape) mtkang/Shutterstock.com; p. 5 kojihirano/Shutterstock.com; p. 7 (top left) Phoo Chan/Shutterstock.com; p. 7 (top right) Anatoliy Lukich/Shutterstock.com; p. 7 (bottom left) Cephas/Wikimedia Commons; p. 7 (bottom right) Flikruploadbot/Wikimedia Commons; p. 8 Victor Tyakht/Shutterstock.com; p. 9 mik ulyannikov/Shutterstock.com; p. 10 Grisha Bruey/Shutterstock.com; p. 11 Michael Woodruff/Shutterstock.com; p. 13 taviphoto/Shutterstock.com; p. 15 Pictureguy/Shutterstock.com; p. 16 Eric Isselee/Shutterstock.com; p. 17 suefeldberg/iStockphoto.com; p. 18 Federico Massa/Shutterstock.com; p. 19 David W. Leindecker/Shutterstock.com; p. 21 SanderMeertinsPhotography/Shutterstock.com; p. 23 Robert L Kothenbeutel/Shutterstock.com; p. 25 Elliotte Rusty Harold/Shutterstock.com; p. 27 Educational Images/Universal Images Group/Getty Images; p. 29 Hatchapong Palurtchaivong/Shutterstock.com.

Printed in the United States of America

CPSIA compliance information: Batch #CW16GS: For further information contact Gareth Stevens, New York, New York at 1-800-542-2595.

CONTENTS

Words in the glossary appear in **bold** type the first time they are used in the text.

IN MY BACKYARD

Long-Lived

A song sparrow might live as long as 11 years in the wild! I wonder how old the birds I see are.

One of my favorite activities is bird-watching. All I need are my eyes. I don't even have to go farther than my backyard! There are so many different types and colors of birds right outside my window. I decided to learn more about them. I bought a **journal** to write down what I find out and to put pictures of birds into.

I really like song sparrows because I always hear them singing. I don't know much about them right now, but I will soon!

Of all the types of birds I know, I think the song sparrow is my favorite. Here's a photo.

SPARROW SPECIES

Sparrow Species

tree sparrow

fox sparrow

lark sparrow

white-crowned sparrow

savannah sparrow

and more!

There are many different species, or types, of sparrows in North America, such as the tree sparrow and fox sparrow. However, I see song sparrows flying around my neighborhood more than any other species.

Song sparrows can be a lot of different colors and sizes, depending on where they live. For example, in the deserts of the Southwest, they look small and pale. On some islands off the Alaska coast, they're large and dark. They're all the same species, though.

These are all song sparrows!

WHERE DO SPARROWS LIVE?

Watch Closely!

Song sparrows pump their tail up and down when they fly.

Song sparrows like to live in all sorts of places. You can find them in **thickets**, on the edge of forests, in fields, and in parks and yards. I live near the ocean. Sparrows love the salt **marshes** here because there are lots of places to build and hide nests.

My backyard has many bushes and trees. It's a perfect area to spy on song sparrows. They like to fly from branch to branch. They always look like they're playing!

Sparrows can easily hide in bushes—even in winter.

9

SONG SPARROW SOUNDS

A song sparrow's song is made up of two to six sharp chirps followed by a trill or a buzz. Each song only lasts a few seconds. Sparrow songs sound different in different places—just like people sound different!

Song sparrows make certain noises and movements to **communicate** with each other. They have a call that means they're excited, another to tell others where they are when they're flying, and yet another that says: "Watch out!" I'm going to listen closely to hear the differences among them.

A HOME FOR A SPARROW

Try, Try Again

Sparrows may make a few nests before they choose one to raise their babies in. Are they just practicing, or are they trying to trick their enemies? We don't know!

Today, I saw two song sparrows flying into and out of the bushes in my backyard. They were carrying grass, bark, and other bits of objects, too. They must be **mates** building a nest!

When sparrows build a nest, they usually hide it in grass or weeds. Nests can be found as high as 10 feet (3 m) up in trees, though. The female sparrow makes the nest, but the male may help carry nest-building matter. The female shapes the nest into a cup.

This sparrow thinks this twig will be perfect for its nest!

13

DINNERTIME!

Sparrow Snacks

- seeds
- grasses
- leaves
- berries
- bugs
- sometimes snails and crabs

I wanted to feed the sparrows that live in my yard, but I realized I didn't know what kind of food they like. Luckily, my new bird book told me all about their favorite meals. Song sparrows mostly eat seeds and grasses, but they may eat bugs, too. Gross! The song sparrows here might even eat crabs from the ocean.

I set up a bird feeder filled with seeds near a tree in my backyard. Sparrows feel safer eating near good cover.

SPARROW EGGS

So Tiny!

Each song sparrow egg is less than 1 inch (2.5 cm) long.

1 inch

I looked out my window today, and I didn't see the sparrows flying around. I think the female sparrow has laid her eggs and is waiting for them to **hatch**.

From my book, I learned song sparrows usually lay between three and five eggs every year. The mother needs to sit on them to keep them warm until they hatch. This is called incubation, and it lasts about 2 weeks. The eggs are a greenish-white color with brown spots. I wish I could see them, but they're hidden!

I don't want to scare the song sparrows, so I'll just look at pictures of a nest in my book.

17

BABY SPARROWS

Wow! The sparrow parents are really racing back and forth today. The eggs must have hatched. My book says the reason the parents are flying around so much is that the babies need to eat—a lot.

Song sparrow nestlings mostly eat **grubs**, caterpillars, flies, and grasshoppers. These help them grow fast until they're ready to leave the nest. Right now, though, they're blind and don't even have feathers. The babies open their eyes 3 or 4 days after they hatch.

Food . . . Fast!

Baby birds need to eat every 15 to 20 minutes after they first hatch!

Nestlings are young birds that aren't able to fly away from the nest yet.

19

READY TO FLY

Today, the baby song sparrows are about 14 days old. They're out of the nest! They hop along the ground now, but they'll be able to fly in just a few days.

The parents are teaching the babies how to find food. The little sparrows seem to just want to be fed, though. They're chirping a lot. In about 3 weeks, the young sparrows will be ready to start life on their own. They grow up so fast!

Another Family

Female song sparrows may lay another group of eggs after the first is hatched.

Both mother and father song sparrows teach their young how to find food.

21

LOOK OUT!

Song Sparrow Enemies:

- birds of prey
- snakes
- raccoons
- cats
- weasels
- skunks

Another thing the sparrows need to learn from their parents is how to stay away from predators. The parents teach them to be watchful. If the young sparrows aren't careful, they could get eaten! Weasels, skunks, cats, and other small predators hunt nestlings. Bigger birds may try to eat adult and baby sparrows, too.

Sparrows get some **protection** from their brownish feathers. The feathers act as **camouflage** and help the birds blend in with tree bark and shadows.

Birds of prey such as this hawk are always on the lookout for a meal.

23

DO SPARROWS MIGRATE?

Some song sparrows **migrate** each year. The farther north a song sparrow lives, the more likely it will migrate south for winter.

I read something strange. The farther north the sparrow lives, the farther south it will migrate. Song sparrows in the middle don't migrate as far. I wonder why.

It gets pretty cold during winter where I live. I think these song sparrows may migrate. I hope they come back to my yard next year!

North America

winter song sparrows
summer song sparrows
year-round song sparrows

WINGED HELPERS

Check the Library!

Nature documentaries are a great way to see birds up close and in action!

Today, I watched a **documentary** on the life of a sparrow. An **ornithologist** (ohr-nuh-THAH-luh-juhst) spoke about how important sparrows and other birds are to their **ecosystem**. They drop seeds on the ground when they eat. They drop seeds by accident when they fly, too. From these seeds, plants grow in new places.

New growth helps keep ecosystems healthy. Imagine if I could help my ecosystem by dropping my food on the ground. Ha!

I thought I was helping sparrows by putting up a bird feeder. Who knew they could help me, too?

27

BIRD-WATCHING PRO

Other Cool Birds I See

cardinals

chickadees

blue jays

hawks

finches

I just looked back through my journal and realized how much I've learned about song sparrows. I know where they live, how they sound, what they eat, and about their nests and eggs. I know who their enemies are, too.

Now that I know so much about my favorite bird, I'm excited to learn about other kinds of birds in my backyard. I bet there are a lot of cool facts about each species. I wonder if I'll have a new favorite bird soon!

My journal will help me sort and remember all my bird facts and photos.

29

GLOSSARY

camouflage: colors or shapes in animals that allow them to blend in with their surroundings

communicate: to share ideas and feelings through sounds and motions

documentary: a movie or TV program presenting information about an issue

ecosystem: all the living things in an area

grub: a wormlike larva of a bug

hatch: to come out of an egg

journal: a book in which one writes down what happens to them or their thoughts

marsh: an area of soft, wet land

mate: one of two animals that come together to produce babies

migrate: to move from one area to another for feeding or having babies

ornithologist: one who studies birds

protection: the act of keeping safe

thicket: a group of bushes or small trees that grow close together

FOR MORE INFORMATION

Books

Amstutz, Lisa J. *House Sparrows*. North Mankato, MN: Capstone Press, 2016.

Cleary, Brian P. *Sparrow, Eagle, Penguin, and Seagull: What Is a Bird?* Minneapolis, MN: Millbrook Press, 2013.

Erickson, Laura. *National Geographic Pocket Guide to the Birds of North America*. Washington, DC: National Geographic, 2013.

Websites

Song Sparrow
www.biokids.umich.edu/critters/Melospiza_melodia/
Find lots of information and pictures of song sparrows.

Song Sparrow
www.allaboutbirds.org/guide/Song_Sparrow/sounds
Listen to the sounds of the song sparrow.

INDEX